THE BEST 50
SHORTBREADS

Barbara Karoff

BRISTOL PUBLISHING ENTERPRISES
San Leandro, California

Printed in the United States of America.

ISBN 1-55867-111-0

Cover design: Frank Paredes
Cover photography: John Benson
Food stylist: Suzanne Carreiro

ABOUT SHORTBREAD

Classic shortbread, well known and well loved, is a cookie of delightful simplicity. It is also versatile. And, I've discovered, in the vernacular of the day, it is extremely user-friendly. Making shortbread is easier than ever. Enjoying it has never been a problem.

Basic shortbread is no more complicated than the right combination of sugar, butter and flour — ingredients almost always ready and waiting in the kitchen. Because this short list of ingredients produces a bland, although rich, buttery and delicious cookie, over the years bakers have added their own personal touches. The following recipes attest to their many creative efforts.

A LITTLE BIT OF HISTORY

Historically, shortbread is associated with Christmas and Hogmanay (New Year's Eve in Scotland). Traditionally, it was, and frequently still is, formed into one large round cookie, notched around the edge to represent the rays of the sun.

The Scots still love shortbread, their sweetest contribution to the world's cuisines. In Edinburgh shortbread is decorated with bits of citrus peel and almonds at holiday time. In Ayrshire it is often enriched with cream and eggs. In the Shetland and Orkney Islands it is flavored with caraway seeds and known as "Bride's Bonn."

The legacy of shortbread as a tea-time favorite remains, but this simple cookie is equally delicious with coffee or milk or wine or champagne. It also complements ice cream, custard, fruit and other simple desserts.

I've discovered, and I'm sure you will too, that a number of favorite recipes, ones in use for years, are really shortbreads even though they are not called by that name. The melt-in-your-mouth, confectioners' sugar-coated balls that are on almost everyone's cookie tray at Christmastime are shortbreads in the round. Rich and tart-sweet lemon bars are fancy shortbreads. Bizcochitos, the traditional Christmas

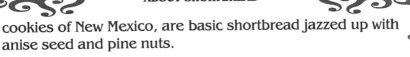
cookies of New Mexico, are basic shortbread jazzed up with anise seed and pine nuts.

BAKING TIPS

Just about any basic butter cookie can rightfully be called a shortbread. Many of these simple cookies developed their own identities when imaginative cooks added fruits, nuts, chocolate, spices, herbs, peels or cheese. Some recipes call for brown sugar instead of granulated or confectioners' sugar, creating a distinctive caramel-like goodness. Others change the type of flour and, like magic, a new cookie is born.

Most shortbreads may be baked in a variety of ways and decorated after baking with frostings, glazes, sprinkles or nuts. They may be dipped in chocolate and chopped nuts. They may be put together sandwich-style with frosting, jam, ground fruits and nuts, or ice cream.

No one need be fussy about the choice of baking pan because shortbread is undemanding and, in most cases, a number of different pans are appropriate. Although I have indicated but one choice for each recipe, if, for instance, the recipe calls for an eight- or nine-inch pie plate, a round or square cake pan works equally well. You may also choose a same size springform pan, a tart pan with or without a removable bottom, or a quiche dish.

Or, you many simply flatten the dough into a free-form circle (or rectangle or square) on a cookie sheet. Or, you may press it into one of the beautifully embossed shortbread molds available in specialty cookware stores. I've also experimented with pressing the dough into individual madeleine or shell molds and have been rewarded with really beautiful little cookies.

Just about any ovenproof mold will work. The point to remember is that the dough should be pressed to a thickness of approximately 1/4 inch. It is important, too, in many of the recipes, to pierce the uncooked dough all over with the tines of a fork to minimize bubbles during baking. It's also a good

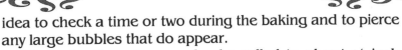
idea to check a time or two during the baking and to pierce any large bubbles that do appear.

Most shortbreads may also be rolled to about 1/4-inch thick on a floured surface and cut with cookie cutters or knife-cut into fingers, diamonds, rectangles or whatevers. Or, they may be rolled out with a patterned rolling pin and then transferred to a cookie sheet.

They may also be formed by hand into small cylinders or balls. The balls may be baked as such or they may be flattened to 1/4-inch thick with a decorative cookie stamp, with the bottom of a glass or with the tines of a fork.

The shortbreads produced by many recipes do exceptional double duty as tart shells and as cheesecake bottoms and may substitute for crumb crust in any recipe. Just be sure that the tart filling you use is compatible with the flavors in the shortbread crust.

USER-FRIENDLY SHORTBREAD

Why can we think of shortbread as user-friendly?

First of all, in most cases, the list of required ingredients is short and simple.

Rarely is it necessary to grease the pan in which the cookies are baked, saving time in preparation and cleanup.

Most shortbreads can be made beautifully in the food processor in less time than it takes to tell about it. Only five recipes in this collection have been clearly identified as inappropriate for the food processor.

I recommend that you use only unsalted (sweet) butter in all the recipes in this collection. Because it spoils more quickly than salted butter, store it in the freezer. As the recipes in this book call for *softened* butter, just set the still-wrapped butter on the kitchen counter for an hour or two and then cut it into 1-inch pieces before using it.

With its simple, flexible rules and consistently delicious results, shortbread is a most accommodating treat.

MASTER SHORTBREAD RECIPE

This recipe makes a wonderful, classic shortbread, very buttery and flaky. It is perfect as is but it also lends itself to many variations.

1 cup butter, softened
½ cup confectioners' sugar
2 cups all-purpose flour
pinch salt

Cream butter and sugar together. Combine flour and salt and add to butter mixture. Blend well. Or, place all ingredients in a food processor and pulse on and off until dough just forms a mass. Press dough evenly into a 9-inch square pan and pierce all over with the tines of a fork. Bake at 350° for 25 to 30 minutes or until golden. Cool in the pan on a rack and cut into rectangles while still warm.

24 cookies

OLD-FASHIONED SHORTBREAD

For a new-fashioned and festive twist, dip half of each cookie in melted chocolate after the cookies have cooled.

1 cup butter, softened
2/3 cup confectioners' sugar
1 tsp. vanilla extract
2 cups all-purpose flour
pinch salt
6 oz. semisweet chocolate, melted with
2 tsp. vegetable oil

Cream butter and sugar together. Add vanilla and blend. Combine flour and salt and add to butter mixture. Blend well. Or, place all ingredients except chocolate and vegetable oil in a food processor and pulse on and off until dough just forms a mass. On a lightly floured surface, roll dough ¼-inch thick. With a cookie cutter, cut into rounds and place

about 1 inch apart on an ungreased cookie sheet. Pierce each cookie several times with the tines of a fork and bake at 350° for about 20 minutes or until they just begin to brown around the edges. Cool cookies on a rack.

Line 2 cookie sheets (not hot ones) with waxed paper. Place melted chocolate mixture in a small bowl. Dip half of each cookie into chocolate, shake off excess and place on cookie sheets until chocolate sets.

24 cookies

SHERRY RAISIN WALNUT SHORTBREAD

With lots of raisins and nuts and a lovely hint of sherry, these cookies are perfect with a cup of tea or coffee or with a bowl of fruit for dessert. The dough must be refrigerated overnight.

½ cup butter, softened
¾ cup granulated sugar
3 tsp. grated orange peel
2 eggs
2 tbs. sherry, any kind
1½ cups all-purpose flour
pinch salt
⅔ cup chopped golden raisins
1⅓ cups chopped walnuts

Cream butter and sugar together. Add orange peel, eggs and sherry; blend. Combine flour and salt and add to butter mixture. Blend well. Add chopped raisins and nuts and mix in. Or, place butter, sugar, orange peel, eggs, sherry, flour and salt in a food processor and pulse on and off until the mixture resembles fine meal. Add raisins and nuts (unchopped for food processor) and continue to pulse until dough just forms a mass. Shape dough into a ball, wrap in plastic wrap and refrigerate overnight.

On a floured surface, roll dough ¼-inch thick. With a sharp knife, cut into rectangles and place on an ungreased cookie sheet 1 inch apart. Bake at 350° for 20 to 25 minutes or until golden. Cool cookies on a rack.

36 cookies

CHOCOLATE CINNAMON SHORTBREAD SLICES

The unbaked dough will keep in the refrigerator for several weeks if tightly wrapped. It's nice to have on hand to bake just a few cookies as needed.

½ cup butter, softened
1 cup granulated sugar
1 tsp. vanilla extract
1 cup all-purpose flour
2 tbs. unsweetened cocoa
½ tsp. baking powder
½ tsp. cinnamon
⅓ cup chopped walnuts or pecans

Cream butter, sugar and vanilla together. Combine flour, cocoa, baking powder and cinnamon; add to butter mixture and blend well. Add nuts and work into dough. Or, place all ingredients except nuts in a food processor and pulse on and off until mixture resembles coarse meal. Add nuts and continue to pulse until dough just forms a mass. Shape dough into 2 cylinders about 1½ inches in diameter, wrap in plastic wrap and refrigerate for 1 hour.

Slice cylinders into ¼-inch-thick cookies and place on ungreased cookie sheets. Bake at 325° for 15 to 18 minutes or until firm. Allow to stand for 5 minutes on sheets before removing to a rack to cool.

42 cookies

MASA HARINA SHORTBREAD

These cookies are a perfect ending to a Mexican meal. Masa harina, the corn flour used in tortillas, is available in many supermarkets or in Latin American markets.

½ cup butter, softened
⅓ cup confectioners' sugar
½ tsp. vanilla extract
¾ cup all-purpose flour
6 tbs. masa harina
pinch salt
1 tbs. minced crystallized ginger

Cream butter and sugar together. Add vanilla and blend. Combine flour, masa harina and salt; add to butter mixture. Blend well. Mix in minced ginger. Or, place all ingredients in a food processor and pulse on and off until dough just forms a mass. Press dough evenly into an 8-inch round pan and pierce all over with the tines of a fork. Bake at 350° for about 20 minutes or until it begins to brown around the edges. Cool in pan for 10 minutes and then cut into wedges while still warm. Transfer cookies to a rack to cool completely.

12 wedges

LINZER SHORTBREAD

Linzer Torte and shortbread are two good things that come together in this delightful recipe.

1 cup butter, softened
1 cup granulated sugar
2 eggs
2 cups all-purpose flour
1 cup ground almonds
½ tsp. cinnamon
½ cup raspberry jam, or more as needed

Cream butter and sugar together. Add eggs and blend well. Combine flour, ground almonds and cinnamon; add to butter mixture. Blend well. Or, place all ingredients, except jam, in a food processor and pulse on and off until dough just forms a mass. On a floured surface, roll ⅔ of the dough into a 12-inch round and place it on an ungreased cookie sheet. Spread jam on top, about ¼-inch thick.

Roll remaining dough ¼-inch thick and cut with a small heart-shaped cookie cutter. Place cutouts attractively on top of jam. Bake at 350° for about 30 minutes or until bottom round is firm and jam is bubbling.

12 servings

CARAWAY SHORTBREAD

In days gone by, caraway seeds were frequently added to shortbread.

½ cup butter, softened
¼ cup granulated sugar
1 cup all-purpose flour
pinch salt
1 tbs. caraway seeds

Cream butter and sugar together. Combine flour, salt and caraway seeds; add to butter mixture. Blend well. Or, place all ingredients in a food processor and pulse on and off until the dough just forms a mass. Press evenly into an 8-inch square pan. Pierce all over with the tines of a fork. Bake at 325° for 25 to 30 minutes or until cookies just begin to color around the edges. Cut into squares while still warm and remove to a rack to cool.

24 cookies

ALMOND SHORTBREAD CUTOUTS

These rich, almond-flavored cookies have been part of my Christmas baking repertoire for many years.

½ cup butter, softened
10 tbs. granulated sugar
¼ tsp. almond extract

¾ cup plus 2 tbs. all-purpose flour
3 oz. almonds with skins, finely ground

Cream butter and sugar together. Add almond extract and blend well. Combine flour and ground almonds; add to butter mixture. Blend well. Or, place all ingredients in a food processor and pulse on and off until dough just forms a mass. On a well-floured surface, roll dough, a small amount at a time, to a thickness of less than ⅛ inch. Cut with a floured cutter and place cookies on an ungreased cookie sheet. Bake at 325° for 8 to 10 minutes or until cookies are firm. Cool on racks.

60 cookies

DATE CHEESE PILLOWS

This cookie presents a most unusual flavor combination. The result is a sweet-savory snack.

7 oz. pitted, chopped dates
¼ cup water
½ cup butter, softened
¼ lb. sharp cheddar cheese, grated (diced
for food processor)
1 cup all-purpose flour

In a small saucepan, cook dates and water over low heat, stirring frequently, until dates are soft and water is absorbed. Set aside to cool.

Cream butter and grated cheddar together. Add flour to butter-cheese mixture. Blend well. Or, place butter, cheese and flour in a food processor and pulse on and off until the dough just forms a mass. Shape into a ball, wrap in plastic wrap and refrigerate for 30 minutes.

On a floured surface, roll half the dough 1/8-inch thick and cut into rounds with a 2-inch cutter. Place on an ungreased cookie sheet and top each round with a scant teaspoon of date mixture. Roll remaining dough 1/8-inch thick and cut with 2-inch cutter. Place a second round on top of date mixture. Gently press together and crimp edges all around with the tines of a fork. Bake at 350° for about 15 minutes or until edges just begin to color. Remove to paper-covered racks to cool.

36 cookies

CRISPY FILLED PILLOWS

The cranberry-orange filling given here is delicious. If you are in a hurry, use prepared jam, marmalade or preserves instead.

1 cup dried cranberries, finely chopped
1 tbs. granulated sugar
2 tbs. orange juice concentrate, undiluted
14 tbs. butter, softened
1 cup granulated sugar
1 egg
1 tsp. almond extract
1 tsp. vanilla extract
1½ cups all-purpose flour
¼ cup cake flour

Combine cranberries with 1 tbs. sugar and orange juice concentrate and set aside.

Cream butter and sugar together. Add egg, almond extract and vanilla and blend. Combine flours and add to butter mixture. Blend well. Or, place butter, sugar, egg, flavorings and flours in a food processor and pulse on and off until dough just forms a mass. Shape into a ball, wrap in plastic wrap and refrigerate for 2 hours.

On a well-floured surface (dough is sticky), roll half the dough 1/8-inch thick and cut into rounds with a 2-inch cutter. Place on an ungreased cookie sheet and top each round with a scant teaspoon of cranberry mixture. Roll remaining dough 1/8-inch thick and cut with 2-inch cutter. Place a second round on top of cranberry mixture. Gently press together and crimp all around with the tines of a fork. Bake at 350° for 8 to 10 minutes or until edges are lightly browned. Cool on a rack.

48 cookies

MACADAMIA NUT
SHORTBREAD CONFECTIONS

*These triple macadamia nut cookies are sinfully elegant.
Other nuts could be substituted.*

¾ cup butter, softened
¾ cup confectioners' sugar
1 cup all-purpose flour
¼ cup cornstarch
¼ cup chopped macadamia nuts
¾ cup ground macadamia nuts
24 macadamia nut halves

Cream butter and sugar together. Combine flour and cornstarch and add to butter mixture. Blend well. Work in 1/4 cup chopped macadamia nuts. Or, place butter, flour, cornstarch, sugar and 1/4 cup macadamia nuts in a food processor and pulse on and off until dough just forms a mass. Shape dough into balls the size of a walnut and roll each ball in ground macadamia nuts. Place on an ungreased cookie sheet and flatten each ball to about 1/4 inch with the tines of a fork. Press a nut half on each cookie and bake at 300° for 25 to 30 minutes or until cookies are lightly browned around the edges. Allow cookies to cool on sheet for 5 minutes and then remove to a rack to cool completely.

24 cookies

VERY ORANGE SHORTBREAD CRISPS

These are very thin, crisp cookies and delicious as they are. They may, however, be made into sandwich cookies with an orange mincemeat filling.

½ cup butter, softened
12 tbs. granulated sugar
3 tbs. orange juice concentrate, undiluted
2 tbs. grated orange peel
1 cup plus 2 tbs. all-purpose flour
pinch salt

Cream butter and sugar together. Add orange juice concentrate and orange peel and mix thoroughly. Combine flour and salt; add to butter mixture and blend well. Or, place all ingredients in a food processor and pulse on and off until dough just forms a mass. Divide dough in half and refrigerate half.

On a floured surface, roll half the dough ¼-inch thick. Cut with a 2-inch round cutter and place rounds 1½ inches apart on ungreased cookie sheets. Repeat with remaining dough. Bake at 325° for about 12 minutes or until cookies begin to brown around the edges. Cool on sheets for 5 minutes and then remove to a paper-covered rack to cool completely.

FILLING FOR SANDWICH COOKIES

3 oz. condensed mincemeat, finely crumbled
2 tbs. orange marmalade
2-3 tbs. hot water

Mix well to a spreading consistency.

36 cookies

WALNUT SHORTBREAD THINS

These buttery cookies could not be easier to make.

1 cup butter, softened
1 cup granulated sugar
1 tsp. vanilla extract

1 egg yolk
2 cups all-purpose flour
1¼ cups chopped walnuts

Cream butter and sugar together. Add vanilla and egg yolk and mix thoroughly. Add flour and blend well. Or, place butter, sugar, vanilla, egg yolk and flour in a food processor and pulse on and off until dough just forms a mass. Remove to a 12-x-16-inch cookie sheet and press dough to an even thickness. Sprinkle nuts on top and gently press into dough. Bake at 350° for 20 to 25 minutes or until lightly browned. Cool on sheet but cut into squares while still warm.

24 cookies

SHORTBREAD GEMS

These have long been tea-time favorites.

1 cup butter, softened
½ cup granulated sugar
2 tsp. vanilla extract
2 cups all-purpose flour

pinch salt
1½ cups finely chopped
 nuts, any kind

Cream butter and sugar together. Add vanilla and mix thoroughly. Combine flour and salt; add to butter mixture and blend well. Or, place all ingredients, except nuts, in a food processor and pulse on and off until dough just forms a mass. Remove dough to a bowl and work in nuts with your fingers. Shape dough into balls the size of a walnut and place 2 inches apart on an ungreased cookie sheet. Bake at 325° for 20 minutes or until cookies just begin to color around the edges. Cool on paper-covered racks.

24 cookies

SPICY LEMON SHORTBREAD

These shortbreads, cut in the traditional wedges, are an interesting change from the more bland variety.

½ cup butter, softened
1 cup confectioners' sugar
1 egg yolk
grated peel of 2 lemons
1½ cups all-purpose flour
¾ tsp. ground cloves
pinch salt
1 egg white
1 tbs. water

Cream butter and sugar together. Add egg yolk and lemon peel and mix thoroughly. Combine flour, cloves and salt; add to butter mixture and blend well. Or, place all ingredients except egg white and water in a food processor and pulse on and off until dough just forms a mass. Press dough evenly into a 9-inch round cake or tart pan. With a knife, score it into 12 wedges and pierce all over with the tines of a fork. Combine egg white and water with a whisk and brush it over dough. Bake at 350° for 20 minutes or until golden. Cool in pan on a rack but cut into wedges while still warm.

VARIATION

Substitute ¾ tsp. freshly grated nutmeg for the cloves and 3 tsp. grated orange peel for the lemon peel.

12 wedges

SHORTBREAD WITH PINE NUTS AND ANISE SEED

This is a classic shortbread with the addition of pine nuts and anise seeds. The result is not unlike the New Mexico Christmas cookie, Bizcochitos.

2/3 cup pine nuts
1/2 cup butter, softened
1/4 cup confectioners' sugar
1 cup flour
pinch salt
1 tsp. anise seeds

In a shallow pan, toast pine nuts in a single layer in a 350° oven for about 6 minutes. Watch carefully. Remove from pan and cool completely.

SWEET SHORTBREADS

Cream butter and sugar together. Combine flour, salt and anise seeds; add to butter mixture and blend well. Or, place all ingredients, except pine nuts, in a food processor and pulse on and off until dough just forms a mass. Turn dough out on a lightly floured surface and, with lightly floured hands, work in pine nuts. Press dough evenly into a 9-inch square pan and pierce it all over with the tines of a fork. Bake at 325° for 25 to 30 minutes or until pale golden. Cool in pan on a rack and cut into squares while still warm.

24 cookies

SHORTBREAD COOKIE BRITTLE

This toffee-like cookie is memorable.

1 cup butter, softened
1 cup granulated sugar
1 tsp. vanilla extract
2 cups all-purpose flour

pinch salt
1 cup semisweet chocolate bits
½ cup finely chopped walnuts

Cream butter and sugar together. Add vanilla and mix thoroughly. Combine flour and salt; add to butter mixture and blend well. Or, place butter, sugar, vanilla, flour and salt in a food processor and pulse on and off until dough just forms a mass. Remove dough to a 15-x-10-x-1-inch jelly roll pan and, with hands, work in chocolate bits and nuts. Press dough evenly into pan. The dough may not cover completely. Bake at 375° for 12 to 15 minutes or until just golden. Watch carefully. Cool in pan on a rack. When cool, break into irregular pieces.

30 cookies

CHOCOLATE ORANGE SHORTBREAD

*Chocolate and orange are a wonderful combination —
delicious with chocolate ice cream or orange sherbet.*

½ cup butter, softened	2 tsp. grated orange peel
½ cup confectioners' sugar	1 cup all-purpose flour
1½ tbs. powdered cocoa	

Cream butter and sugar together. Add cocoa and orange peel and mix thoroughly. Add flour and blend well. Or, place all ingredients in a food processor and pulse on and off until dough just forms a mass. Lightly butter a ceramic shortbread mold or an 8-inch round cake pan and press dough evenly on the bottom. Pierce the surface all over with the tines of a fork and bake at 325° for 30 to 35 minutes or until the edges just begin to darken. Cool in pan for 10 minutes. Cut into wedges while still warm and cool completely on a rack.

12 wedges

RAINBOW SHORTBREAD BALLS

Decked out in bright red and green, these are an all-time Christmas favorite. Use other colors for other seasons.

1 cup butter, softened
1/4 cup confectioners' sugar
2 tsp. vanilla extract
1 tbs. water

2 cups all-purpose flour
1 cup chopped pecans
colored sugar for rolling

Cream butter and sugar together. Add vanilla and water and mix thoroughly. Add flour and blend well. Work pecans into dough. Or, place all ingredients, except colored sugar, in a food processor and pulse on and off until dough just forms a mass. Shape dough into balls the size of a walnut and roll each ball in colored sugar, coating it all over. Place cookies on an ungreased cookie sheet and bake at 300° for 20 minutes or until firm. Cool thoroughly before removing from cookie sheet.

36 cookies

BROWN SUGAR SHORTBREAD

This is a delicious simple cookie to serve with tea or with a fruit dessert.

½ cup butter, softened
¼ cup brown sugar, firmly
  packed

2 cups all-purpose flour
½ tsp. freshly grated nutmeg
pinch salt

Cream butter and sugar together. Combine flour, nutmeg and salt; add to butter mixture and blend well. Or, place all ingredients in a food processor and pulse on and off until dough just forms a mass. On a lightly floured surface, roll dough ½-inch thick. Cut with round (or other shape) cutter and place cookies on an ungreased cookie sheet. Pierce each cookie several times with the tines of a fork. Bake at 300° for 25 minutes or until cookies just begin to color around the edges. Remove to a rack to cool.

24 cookies

ORANGE RAISIN NUT SHORTBREAD

The special ingredients in these cookies add up to a superior flavor combination.

> ½ cup chopped golden raisins
> ⅓ cup orange juice
> ¾ cup butter, softened
> ¼ cup granulated sugar
> grated peel of 1 orange
> 1½ cups all-purpose flour
> pinch salt
> ⅓ cup chopped walnuts

In a small saucepan, heat raisins and orange juice to boiling. Reduce heat and simmer until liquid is reduced to 1 tbs. Set aside and cool completely.

Cream butter and sugar together. Add orange peel and raisin water; blend. Combine flour and salt; add to butter mixture and blend well. Add raisins and chopped nuts and mix thoroughly. Or, place butter, sugar, orange peel, flour and salt in a food processor and pulse on and off until dough just forms a mass. Add raisins with their liquid and nuts and pulse just enough to combine. Turn dough onto a lightly greased cookie sheet and pat it into an 8- to 9-inch round. With a sharp knife, score into 12 wedges and pierce each wedge several times with the tines of a fork.

Bake at 300° for 35 minutes or until golden and firm in the center. Cut wedges through while still warm and cool completely on cookie sheet on a rack.

12 wedges

DOUBLE GINGER SHORTBREAD

The spicy tang of ginger goes well with shortbread.

½ cup butter, softened
⅓ cup granulated sugar
1¼ cup all-purpose flour

½ tsp. ground ginger
3 tbs. minced crystallized
  ginger

Cream butter and sugar together. Combine flour and ground ginger; add to butter mixture and blend well. Work crystallized ginger into dough. Or, place all ingredients, except crystallized ginger, in a food processor and pulse on and off until dough just begins to form a mass. Add crystallized ginger and continue to pulse until dough forms a mass. Press dough evenly into a 9-inch pie pan and, with a sharp knife, score into 12 wedges. Pierce each wedge several times with the tines of a fork. Bake at 325° for 40 minutes or until golden and firm in the center. Cut through into wedges while still warm and cool completely in pan on a rack.

12 wedges

SHORTBREAD SURPRISE BALLS

There's a hazelnut surprise hidden inside each ball.

48 whole hazelnuts
1 cup butter, softened
¾ cup confectioners' sugar
2 tsp. vanilla extract

2½ cups all-purpose flour
pinch salt
confectioners' sugar for rolling cookies, about 1½ cups

In a shallow pan, toast hazelnuts in a single layer in a 350° oven for about 10 minutes. Remove from pan and cool.

Cream butter and sugar together. Add vanilla and blend. Combine flour and salt; add to butter mixture and blend well. Or, place butter, sugar, vanilla, flour and salt in a food processor and pulse on and off until dough just forms a mass. Form into walnut-sized balls and place a whole hazelnut inside each. Place on an ungreased cookie sheet and bake at 400° for 10 to 12 minutes or until just firm. Do not allow to brown. Cool slightly on a rack and then roll each ball in confectioners' sugar while still warm.

48 cookies

COCONUT SHORTBREAD COQUILLES

Shell molds or madeleine tins produce a decorative cookie. Or, use an 8-inch cake pan. Be sure to use unsweetened coconut, which is available at health food stores.

½ cup butter, softened
4 tbs. granulated sugar
1 tsp. vanilla extract

1 cup all-purpose flour
pinch salt
2 cups unsweetened coconut

Cream butter, sugar and vanilla together. Combine flour and salt; add to butter mixture and blend well. Add coconut and work into dough. Or, place all ingredients in a food processor and pulse on and off until dough just forms a mass. Press dough into molds, filling not quite full. Refrigerate for 15 minutes. Bake at 350° for 25 minutes or until golden. Cool in mold on a rack for 5 minutes and then tap mold to release cookies. Cool completely on a rack.

16 cookies

SUGAR AND SPICE SHORTBREAD

This is a spiced-up version of a traditional shortbread.

1¼ cups butter, softened	2 tsp. cinnamon
¾ cup granulated sugar	½ tsp. ground cardamom
1 tsp. vanilla extract	½ tsp. ground ginger
3 cups all-purpose flour	¾ tsp. ground allspice
pinch salt	1 tbs. granulated sugar

Cream butter, sugar and vanilla together. Combine flour, salt and spices; add to butter mixture and blend well. Or, place all ingredients, except 1 tbs. sugar, in a food processor and pulse on and off until dough just forms a mass. Press dough evenly into an 8-inch round pan or shortbread mold. With a sharp knife, score into 12 wedges and pierce each wedge in several places with the tines of a fork. Sprinkle with 1 tbs. sugar. Bake at 350° for about 1 hour or until the cookie is firm but not brown. Cut through wedges while still warm. Cool in the pan on a rack.

12 wedges

CINNAMON SHORTBREAD BALLS

These buttery balls have a lovely cinnamon flavor.

½ cup butter, softened
¼ cup confectioners' sugar
½ tsp. vanilla extract
1 cup all-purpose flour

pinch salt
¼ tsp. cinnamon
½ cup confectioners' sugar
½ tsp. cinnamon

Cream butter and ¼ cup confectioners' sugar together. Add vanilla and blend. Combine flour with salt and ¼ tsp. cinnamon; add to butter mixture and blend well. Or, place butter, ¼ cup confectioners' sugar, ¼ tsp. cinnamon, salt, vanilla and flour in a food processor and pulse on and off until dough just forms a mass. Wrap dough in plastic wrap and refrigerate for 1 hour.

In a small dish, combine remaining sugar and cinnamon. Form dough into walnut-sized balls balls and roll in cinnamon sugar. Place on an ungreased cookie sheet and bake at 350° for 15 to 20 minutes or until firm. Cool on a rack.

30 cookies

CARDAMOM BUCKWHEAT SHORTBREAD

These cookies are unusual and a delicious treat for buckwheat lovers. They burn easily, so watch carefully.

½ cup butter, softened
½ cup confectioners' sugar
½ cup buckwheat flour

½ cup all-purpose flour
½ tsp. ground cardamom

Cream butter and sugar together. Combine flours and cardamom; add to butter mixture and blend well. Or, place all ingredients in a food processor and pulse on and off until dough just forms a mass. Shape dough into 2 cylinders, each 1½ inches in diameter, wrap separately in plastic wrap and refrigerate for 1 hour.

Slice cylinders into cookies ⅓-inch thick and place them on ungreased cookie sheets. Bake at 325° for 15 minutes or until cookies are firm. Cool on racks.

24 cookies

CHOCOLATE PECAN SHORTBREAD

This recipe begins as a classic shortbread, but once the topping is spread on, it's almost like a chocolate pecan pie!

½ cup butter, softened
¼ cup granulated sugar
1½ cups flour
¾ cup light corn syrup
3 squares (1 oz. each) semisweet chocolate
¾ cup granulated sugar
2 eggs, lightly beaten
1 tsp. vanilla extract
1 cup coarsely chopped pecans

Cream butter and ¼ cup sugar together. Add flour and blend well. Or, place flour, ¼ cup sugar and butter in a food processor and pulse on and off until dough just forms a mass. Press dough evenly into the lightly greased bottom of a 9-inch springform pan and bake at 350° for 20 minutes.

In a saucepan, combine corn syrup and chocolate over low heat until chocolate is melted. Remove from heat and stir in ¾ cup sugar, eggs and vanilla. Mix well and stir in pecans. Pour this mixture over hot crust and continue to bake at 350° for 30 minutes or until topping is firm around the edges and slightly soft in the center. Cool in pan on a rack. Cut when completely cool.

8-10 wedges

WHOLE WHEAT HAZELNUT SHORTBREAD

These rich, nutty cookies are wonderful with ice cream.

¾ cup hazelnuts
½ cup butter, softened

½ cup granulated sugar
1 cup whole wheat flour

In a shallow pan, toast hazelnuts in a single layer in a 350° oven for about 10 minutes. Remove from pan, cool and chop coarsely.

Cream butter and sugar together. Add flour and blend well. Add hazelnuts and work into dough. Or, place butter, sugar and flour in a food processor and pulse on and off until mixture resembles coarse meal. Add toasted hazelnuts (no need to chop first) and continue to pulse until dough just forms a mass and nuts are coarsely chopped. Press dough evenly into a 9-inch springform pan and bake for 15 minutes or until cookie begins to pull away from sides of pan. Cut cookie into wedges while still warm and cool on a rack.

12 wedges

WALNUT SHORTBREAD FINGERS

A light dusting of cinnamon and sugar adds extra interest to these delicious cookies.

½ cup butter, softened	1 cup chopped walnuts
½ cup granulated sugar	1 tbs. granulated sugar
1 cup all-purpose flour	½ tsp. cinnamon

Cream butter and ½ cup sugar together. Add flour and blend well. Add nuts and work into dough. Or, place butter, sugar and flour in a food processor and pulse on and off until mixture resembles coarse meal. Add walnuts and continue to pulse until nuts are finely chopped and dough holds together. Press dough evenly into a 9-inch square pan and pierce all over with the tines of a fork. Combine 1 tbs. sugar and cinnamon and sprinkle over dough. Bake at 350° for 25 minutes or until golden. Cut into fingers while still warm, and cool in the pan.

30 cookies

PEANUT SHORTBREAD

These cookies are a peanut lover's delight.

½ cup butter, softened
2 tbs. peanut butter
½ cup granulated sugar
1 egg yolk
1 tsp. vanilla extract

½ cup plus 3 tbs. all-
  purpose flour
½ cup rolled oats
½ cup finely chopped un-
  salted dry roasted peanuts

Cream butter, peanut butter and sugar together. Add egg yolk and vanilla and blend. Combine flour and rolled oats; add to butter mixture and blend well. Or, place all ingredients, except peanuts, in a food processor and pulse on and off until dough just forms a mass. Press dough evenly into an ungreased 9-inch square pan. Sprinkle with chopped peanuts and press them gently into dough. Bake at 300° for 25 to 30 minutes or until golden. Cut into squares while still warm and cool in pan on a rack.

24 cookies

POPPY SEED LEMON SHORTBREAD

Poppy seeds and lemons combine wonderfully.

1½ tbs. poppy seeds
enough milk to cover seeds
½ cup butter, softened
½ cup confectioners' sugar

1½ tbs. grated lemon peel
½ tsp. vanilla extract
1 cup all-purpose flour
pinch salt

Soak poppy seeds in milk to cover for 20 minutes. Drain well through coffee filter paper and discard milk. Cream butter and sugar together. Add lemon peel and vanilla; blend. Combine flour and salt; add to butter mixture and blend well. Add poppy seeds and mix well. Or, place all ingredients, including drained poppy seeds, in a food processor and pulse on and off until dough just forms a mass. Press dough evenly into an 8-inch square pan and bake at 300° for 30 to 35 minutes or until pale golden. Cool in pan on a rack for 10 minutes and cut into squares while still warm. Cool completely in pan.

24 cookies

VANILLA SHORTBREAD WEDGES

Bake these traditional shortbreads in a decorative ceramic mold or in a 9-inch pie plate.

1½ cups butter, softened
1 cup granulated sugar
2 tsp. vanilla extract

3½ cups all-purpose flour
pinch salt

Cream butter and sugar together. Add vanilla and blend. Combine flour and salt; add to butter mixture and blend well. Or, place all ingredients in a food processor and pulse on and off until dough just forms a mass. Press dough evenly into a shortbread mold or a 9-inch pie pan and pierce all over with the tines of a fork. Bake at 350° for 20 minutes or until golden. Cool on a rack and cut into wedges while still warm.

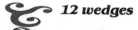

12 wedges

HAZELNUT SHORTBREAD HEARTS

These Valentine hearts are special in any shape on any day.

1¼ cups hazelnuts with
skins
¾ cup butter, softened

½ cup plus 2 tbs. granu-
lated sugar
1¼ cups all-purpose flour

In a shallow pan, toast hazelnuts in a single layer in a 350° oven for 10 minutes. Remove from pan to cool. Chop finely. Cream butter and sugar together. Add flour and blend well. Work hazelnuts into dough. Or, place all ingredients, including *whole* hazelnuts, in a food processor and pulse on and off until dough just forms a mass. Shape into 2 or 3 balls. On a lightly floured surface, roll dough ¼-inch thick. Cut with a heart (or other) cutter and place cookies on an ungreased cookie sheet. Bake at 350° for 15 minutes or until cookies are pale golden. Cool on a rack.

24 cookies

CRUNCHY BROWN SUGAR WAFERS

These simple cookies become delightfully crunchy as they cool.

½ cup butter, softened
10 tbs. brown sugar, lightly packed

½ tsp. vanilla extract
1¼ cups all-purpose flour

Cream butter and sugar together. Add vanilla and mix thoroughly. Add flour and blend well. Or, place all ingredients in a food processor and pulse on and off until dough just forms a mass. Shape dough into a ball, wrap in plastic wrap and refrigerate for 1 hour.

On a lightly floured surface, roll dough ¼-inch thick and cut with cookie cutters, or into squares with a knife. Place on an ungreased cookie sheet. Bake at 300° for 35 to 40 minutes or until firm to the touch. Cool on racks.

36 cookies

LEMON THYME SHORTBREAD

These cookies are not overly sweet, but are very buttery and fragrant with an elusive hint of thyme.

½ cup butter, softened
¼ cup confectioners' sugar
1 cup all-purpose flour

pinch salt
1 tbs. grated lemon peel
1 tsp. dried thyme

Cream butter and sugar together. Combine flour, salt, lemon peel and thyme; add to butter mixture and blend well. Or, place all ingredients in a food processor and pulse on and off until dough just forms a mass. Press dough evenly into an 8-inch pan and pierce all over with the tines of a fork. Bake at 325° for 25 to 30 minutes or until just beginning to brown around the edges. Cut into squares or diamonds while still warm and remove cookies to a rack to cool.

24 cookies

ORANGE-GLAZED SHORTBREAD SQUARES

A simple orange glaze turns these cookies into a special treat.

½ cup butter, softened
¼ cup granulated sugar
1 tbs. orange juice
2 tsp. grated orange peel
1¼ cups all-purpose flour
pinch salt
Glaze, follows

Cream butter and sugar together. Add orange juice and orange peel and mix thoroughly. Combine flour and salt; add to butter mixture and blend well. Or, place all cookie ingredients in a food processor and pulse on and off until dough just forms a mass. Press dough evenly into a 9-inch square pan and pierce all over with the tines of a fork. Bake at 325°

for 40 minutes or until pale golden. Cool slightly in the pan and then drizzle with *Glaze*. Cut into rectangles while still warm and then cool completely in pan.

GLAZE
½ cup confectioners' sugar
½ tsp. grated orange peel
2 tbs. orange juice

Stir all ingredients together until smooth.

48 cookies

RUM RAISIN SHORTBREAD

These cookies require planning ahead. The raisins need to soak for several hours or overnight.

½ cup chopped golden raisins
¼ cup dark rum
½ cup butter, softened
¼ cup confectioners' sugar
1 cup all-purpose flour
⅛ tsp. baking powder
pinch salt

Soak raisins in rum for several hours or overnight. When ready to use, drain well.

58

Cream butter and sugar together. Combine flour, baking powder and salt; add to butter mixture and blend well. Add raisins and work into dough. Or, place all ingredients, including raisins, in a food processor and pulse on and off until dough just forms a mass. Shape dough into a ball, wrap in plastic wrap and refrigerate for 2 hours.

On a lightly floured surface, roll dough ½-inch thick. Cut into rounds with a cookie cutter and place 1 inch apart on an ungreased cookie sheet. Press scraps together and reroll. Bake at 375° for 15 minutes or until lightly browned. Cool on racks.

24 cookies

SESAME SHORTBREAD

Sesame seeds add a delightful flavor and crunch.

3 tbs. sesame seeds
1 cup butter, softened
½ cup granulated sugar
2 cups all-purpose flour
½ tsp. ground cardamom

Toast sesame seeds in a shallow pan in a 400° oven for 10 minutes or until golden. Shake pan several times to prevent burning. Remove from pan and cool.

Cream butter and sugar together. Combine flour, cardamom and sesame seeds; add to butter mixture and blend well. Or, place all ingredients in a food processor and pulse on and off until dough just forms a mass. Shape dough into 2 cylinders 1½ inches in diameter, wrap in plastic wrap and refrigerate for 30 minutes. Cut into ¼-inch-thick slices and place on an ungreased cookie sheet. Bake at 375° for 15 minutes or until lightly browned around the edges. Cool on racks.

72 cookies

TAHINI SHORTBREAD

These cookies are most unusual and very appealing.

¾ cup butter, softened
½ cup tahini (sesame paste)
1¼ cups brown sugar,
  lightly packed

pinch salt
2 cups all-purpose flour
½ cup chopped pecans

Cream butter, tahini and sugar together. Add flour to butter mixture and blend well. Or, place all ingredients in a food processor and pulse on and off until dough just forms a mass. The dough will be very stiff. Divide dough in half and press it evenly into two 9-inch pie plates. Pierce all over with the tines of a fork. Bake at 375° for 15 minutes or until the edges are just golden. Cut into wedges while still warm. Cool on racks.

24 wedges

LEMON FANTASY SHORTBREADS

You can't eat too many of these special cookies at one sitting. They are very rich, and oh, so delicious.

½ cup butter, softened
¼ cup confectioners' sugar
1 cup all-purpose flour
2 eggs
¾ cup granulated sugar
3 tbs. lemon juice
2 tbs. all-purpose flour
½ tsp. baking powder

Cream butter and confectioners' sugar together. Add flour to butter mixture and blend well. Or, place butter, confectioners' sugar and 1 cup flour in a food processor and pulse on and off until dough just forms a mass. Press dough evenly into an 8-inch square pan and bake at 350° for 12 to 15 minutes or until golden.

With an electric mixer, beat eggs until light and foamy. Beat in 3/4 cup granulated sugar and lemon juice and beat for 8 minutes at medium speed. Sift in 2 tbs. flour and baking powder and stir to combine. Pour this mixture over hot shortbread and bake at 350° for 20 minutes or until golden. Cool in pan on a rack. Cut into small squares when cool.

24 cookies

ANISE SUGAR SHORTBREAD

Do not make these cookies in a food processor. If you are fond of anise, you'll love them.

¾ cup butter, softened
¾ cup granulated sugar
1 tbs. anise seed, crushed
1 egg
½ tsp. anise extract

2 cups all-purpose flour
¼ tsp. baking soda
pinch salt
sugar for rolling, about ¾ cup

In a large bowl, cream together butter and sugar. Add anise seed, egg and anise extract and combine well. In another bowl combine flour, baking soda and salt and add to creamed mixture in ½-cup increments. With floured hands, roll dough into walnut-sized balls. Roll balls in sugar. Place on an ungreased cookie sheet and flatten to ¼ inch with the bottom of a glass. Bake at 400° for 6 to 9 minutes or until just browned around the edges. Cool on racks.

60 cookies

PECAN BALLS

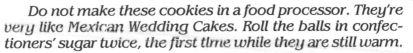

Do not make these cookies in a food processor. They're very like Mexican Wedding Cakes. Roll the balls in confectioners' sugar twice, the first time while they are still warm.

½ cup butter, softened
2 tbs. confectioners' sugar
1 tsp. vanilla extract
pinch salt

1 cup all-purpose flour
1 cup chopped pecans
confectioners' sugar for
   rolling, about 1½ cups

In a medium bowl, cream butter and sugar together. Add vanilla, salt and flour and, when thoroughly combined, add pecans. Roll dough into balls the size of a walnut and place on an ungreased cookie sheet. Bake at 350° for 15 to 20 minutes or until firm. Roll each ball in confectioners' sugar while still warm. Cool on racks and roll in sugar again.

48 cookies

COFFEE SHORTBREAD DIPS

Do not make these cookies in a food processor. These wonderful shortbread fingers are flavored with coffee and dipped in chocolate and nuts. Who could ask for anything more?

1/2 cup butter, softened
3/4 cup brown sugar, firmly packed
2 tsp. instant coffee powder
1/4 cup cream
2 cups all-purpose flour
1/2 tsp. baking powder
pinch salt
1/2 cup semisweet chocolate bits
2 tbs. sugar
2 tbs. water
3/4 cup finely chopped nuts

In a large bowl, cream butter and sugar together until well blended. Dissolve coffee powder in cream; add to butter mixture and mix well. In a small bowl, combine flour, baking powder and salt and blend into butter mixture. Cover bowl with plastic wrap and refrigerate for 1 hour.

Shape dough into fingers about 3 inches long and bake on an ungreased cookie sheet at 375° for 12 to 15 minutes or until firm. Cool on a rack.

In a small pan, melt chocolate, 2 tbs. sugar and water together over very low heat, stirring and taking care not to burn. Dip one end of each cookie into chocolate and then into chopped nuts. Set on a rack until chocolate hardens.

36 cookies

CHOCOLATE NUT CRISPIES

Do not make these cookies in a food processor. These are very thin, delicious cookies.

2 squares (1 oz. each) unsweetened chocolate
½ cup butter
½ cup all-purpose flour
1 cup sugar

pinch salt
2 eggs, well beaten
1 tsp. vanilla extract
1 cup finely chopped nuts

In a medium pan, melt chocolate and butter together over low heat. Remove from heat. In a small bowl, combine flour, sugar and salt and add them to chocolate mixture. Stir in eggs and vanilla and blend in nuts. Spread dough evenly on a lightly greased 15-x-10-x-1-inch jelly roll pan and bake at 400° for 10 to 12 minutes. Cut into squares while still warm. Cool in the pan on a rack.

30 cookies

SHORTBREAD TOFFEE COOKIES

Do not make these rich cookies in a food processor.

½ cup butter
½ cup brown sugar, firmly
  packed
½ cup granulated sugar
1 egg yolk

pinch salt
½ cup all-purpose flour
½ cup rolled oats
6 oz. chocolate bits
½ cup chopped walnuts

In a medium pan, combine butter and sugars. Heat over low heat until butter is melted. Add egg yolk, salt, flour and rolled oats and mix well. Press mixture evenly into a lightly greased 9-x-13-inch pan and bake at 325° for 25 minutes. Remove pan to a rack.

In a small pan, melt chocolate bits over very low heat. Be careful — they burn easily. Use chocolate to frost cookies. Sprinkle with chopped nuts. When chocolate sets (it takes quite awhile), cut cookies into small squares before they cool.

30 cookies

SHORTBREAD TART SHELL

This short, sweet crust is perfect with fruit tarts.

½ cup butter, softened
¼ cup confectioners' sugar
½ tsp. vanilla extract
pinch salt

3 tbs. cornstarch
¾ cup plus 2 tbs. all-
purpose flour

Cream butter and sugar together. Add vanilla and blend. Combine salt, cornstarch and flour and add to butter mixture. Blend well. Or, place all ingredients in a food processor and pulse on and off until dough just forms a mass. Add 1 tbs. more flour if dough is too sticky. Shape dough into a ball, wrap in plastic wrap and refrigerate for 1 hour.

Press dough evenly on bottom and sides of an 8-inch tart pan with a removable bottom. Pierce all over with the tines of a fork and bake at 300° for 15 to 20 minutes or until shell just begins to color. Cool on a rack before filling.

one 9-inch tart shell

CHEESE SHORTBREAD FINGERS

These cheesy fingers are perfect for snacking and great to have on hand. They keep well in the freezer.

1/2 cup butter, softened
1/2 lb. sharp cheddar or blue cheese
1 tsp. Worcestershire sauce
1/2 tsp. cayenne pepper
13/4 cups all-purpose flour

Cream butter, cheese, Worcestershire sauce and cayenne together. Add flour and blend well. Or, place all ingredients in a food processor and pulse on and off until dough just forms a mass. Pinch off a piece of dough and roll it into a finger about 3 inches long. Place on an ungreased cookie sheet and bake at 300° for 20 to 25 minutes or until firm and lightly browned.

30 fingers

CURRIED CHEDDAR CHUTNEY COOKIES

If you do not care for chutney, simply flatten the balls with the tines of a fork and bake as crispy wafers.

¼ cup butter, softened
¼ lb. sharp cheddar
  cheese, grated
1 egg

1 cup all-purpose flour
¾ tsp. curry powder
3-4 tbs. Major Grey's chutney, chopped if large pieces

Cream butter and cheese together. Add egg and blend. Add flour and curry powder and blend well. Or, place flour, cheese, butter and curry powder in a food processor and pulse on and off until mixture resembles coarse meal. Add egg and continue to pulse until dough just forms a mass. Form dough into walnut-sized balls and place on an ungreased cookie sheet. Make a small hollow in the center of each ball with your thumb. Place about ½ tsp. chutney in each hollow and bake at 425° for 12 to 15 minutes or until golden. Cool on racks.

18 cookies

APRICOT CURRY SHORTBREAD

Not quite sweet and not quite savory — just delicious.

½ cup butter, softened
1 cup brown sugar, firmly
  packed
1 egg
1½ cups all-purpose flour
1½ tsp. curry powder

½ tsp. baking powder
¼ tsp. baking soda
pinch salt
1 cup finely chopped dried
  apricots

Cream butter, sugar and egg together. Combine dry ingredients, except apricots; add to butter mixture and blend well. Work chopped apricots into dough. Or, place all ingredients in a food processor and pulse on and off until dough just forms a mass. Shape into a ball, wrap in plastic wrap and refrigerate for 2 hours. Roll dough into walnut-sized balls. On an ungreased cookie sheet, flatten each ball to ¼ inch with the tines of a fork. Bake for 10 to 12 minutes or until lightly browned. Cool on racks.

50 cookies

PISTACHIO BLUE CHEESE WAFERS

These are delicious savory appetizers. If pistachios are unavailable, walnuts or pecans work well.

½ cup butter, softened
2 cups crumbled blue
  cheese

few drops Tabasco Sauce
1 cup all-purpose flour
1 cup pistachio nuts

Cream butter, cheese and Tabasco together. Add flour and blend well. Work nuts into dough. Or, place all ingredients in a food processor and pulse on and off until dough just forms a mass. Divide dough in half and form it into 2 cylinders, each 1 inch in diameter. Wrap cylinders in plastic wrap and refrigerate for 1 hour. With a sharp knife, cut cylinders into ¼-inch slices and place slices on an ungreased cookie sheet. Bake at 350° for 10 to 12 minutes or until golden around the edges. Cool on a paper-covered rack.

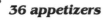

36 appetizers

INDEX

Almond shortbread cutouts 19
Anise sugar shortbread 64
Apricot curry shortbreads 72

Baking pans 3, 4
Baking tips 3-5
Bizcochitos 2, 32
Bride's Bonn 2
Brown sugar shortbread 37
Butter, unsalted 6

Caraway shortbread 18
Cardamom buckwheat short-
    bread 45
Cheese
    curried cheddar chutney
        cookies 71

date pillows 20
    shortbread fingers 70
Chocolate
    cinnamon shortbread slices
        12
    coffee shortbread dips 66
    nut crispies 68
    old-fashioned shortbread 8
    orange shortbread 35
    pecan shortbread 46
    shortbread cookie brittle 34
    shortbread toffee cookies 69
Cinnamon shortbread balls 44
Coconut shortbread coquilles
    42
Coffee shortbread dips 66
Crispy filled pillows 22

Crumb crust substitute 5
Crunchy brown sugar wafers
 54
Curried cheddar chutney
 cookies 71
Cutouts
 almond shortbread 19
 brown sugar shortbread 37
 crispy filled pillows 22
 crunchy brown sugar wafers
  54
 date cheese pillows 20
 hazelnut shortbread hearts
  53
 Linzer shortbread 16
 old-fashioned shortbread 8
 rum raisin shortbread 58
 sherry raisin walnut shortbread 10

very orange shortbread
 crisps 26

Date cheese pillows 20
Double ginger shortbread 40

Filling
 cranberry orange 22
 date 20
 mincemeat and marmalade
  27

Hazelnut
 shortbread hearts 53
 shortbread surprise balls 41
 whole wheat shortbread 48
History 1, 2

Lemon
 fantasy shortbreads 62

Lemon, continued
   shortbread, spicy 30
   thyme shortbread 55
Linzer shortbread 16

Macadamia nut shortbread
   confections 24
Masa harina shortbread 14
Master shortbread recipe 7
Mexican wedding cakes 65
Molds 4

Old-fashioned shortbread 8
Orange
   raisin nut shortbread 38
   very, shortbread crisps 26
   glazed shortbread squares
    56

Peanut shortbread 50

Pecan balls 65
Pine nuts and anise seed
   shortbread 32
Pistachio blue cheese wafers
   73
Poppy seed lemon shortbread
   51

Rainbow shortbread balls 36
Rum raisin shortbread 58

Savory
   apricot curry shortbreads 72
   cheese shortbread fingers
    70
   curried cheddar chutney
    cookies 71
   pistachio blue cheese
    wafers 73
Sesame shortbread 60

Shaping douugh 4,5
Sherry raisin walnut short-
    bread 10
Shortbread cookie brittle 34
Shortbread gems 29
Shortbread surprise balls 41
Shortbread toffee cookies 69
Sugar and spice shortbread 43

Tahini shortbread 61
Tart shells 5
    shortbread 70

Vanilla shortbread wedges 52

Walnut shortbread
    fingers 49
    thins 28
Whole wheat hazelnut short-
    bread 48